For Kids Only

Grade 1

Assessment Booklet

4

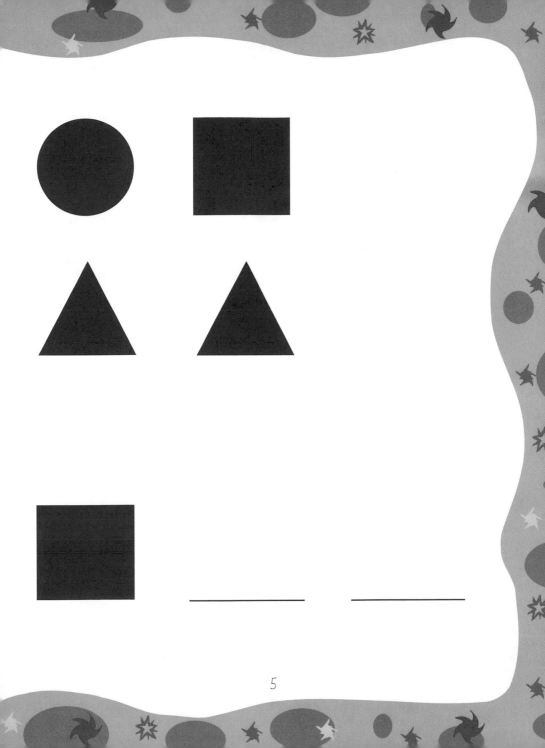

5

5

2 4 5

1 7 10

3 8

6 9

12 18 11

26 43 38

57 69 99

14 15

50 33

74 81

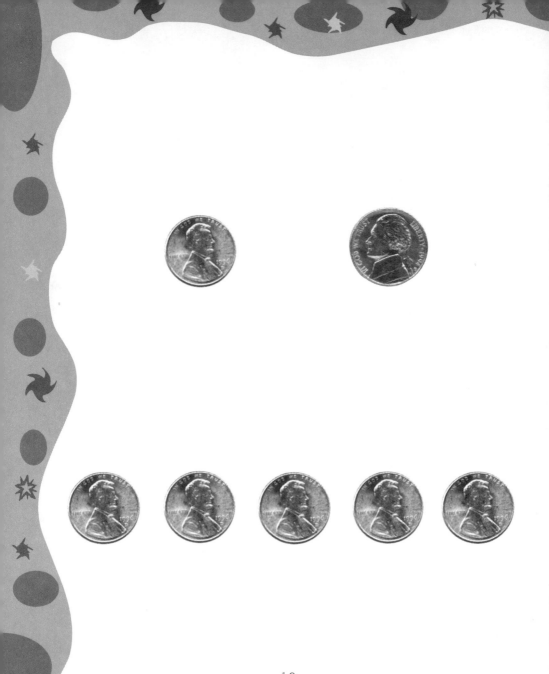

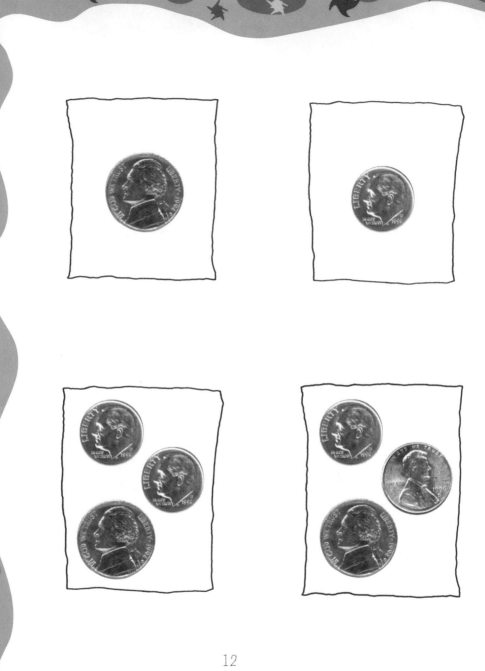

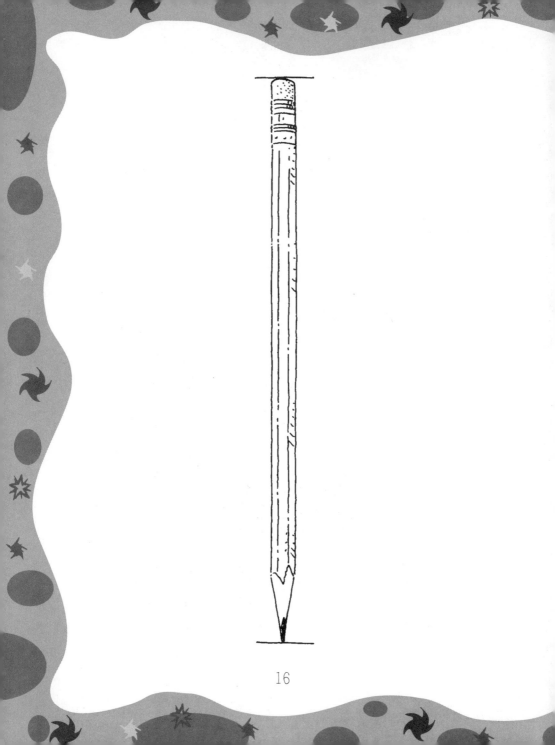

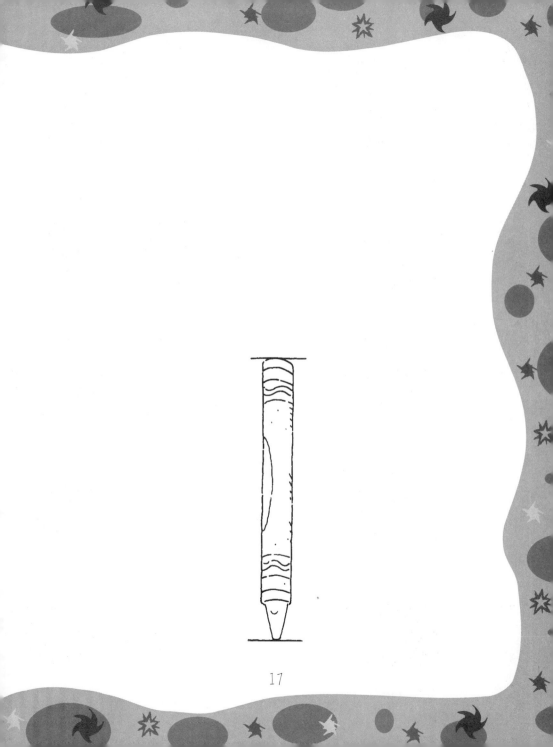

86   3

20

A Q Z

E D C

T P H

B G U

W S X

R F V

N Y J M

K I L O

k q z w

n d c l

t p h y

a e u i

Pat Pet Pit

s   x

r   f   v

j   m   g

o

Pot Hut

We eat.

We jump.

We brush.

We jump.

We dress.

We jump.

We run!

Tom was on his way home.

He saw a cat in a tree.

"I will help you," said Tom.

Tom climbed up the tree.

The cat jumped down.

"You are a funny cat," said Tom.

Pam and Mike like to ride
their bikes.

They can ride them in the park.

They can ride them on the sidewalk
in front of their house.

They would like to ride their
bikes into town.

But they need to wait until they
are older.

The streets going into town
are too busy.

Beth saw a shovel near the fence. What was it doing there? Beth picked up the shovel and began to dig. She liked digging. It was fun. She dug all afternoon. Beth climbed up out of the hole and looked down.

"Oh, no!" What would her mother and her father say when they saw the big hole in the yard?

Just then her mother came out of the garage carrying a little tree.

"Why, Beth," she said. "I was going to dig a hole in that very place. You did all the work for me!"

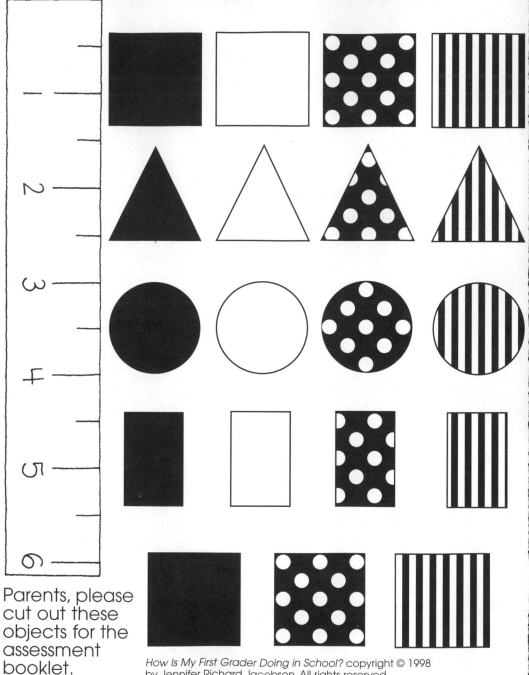

Parents, please cut out these objects for the assessment booklet.